ary's f

(tribe of Juda)
descendant of David
Mary's Grandfather

JACOB
Mary's Uncle
born 45 years
before Jesus

JAMES
ry's Brother-in-Law
born 15 years
before Jesus

MARY
CLEOPHAS
Mary's Sister-in-Law
born 10 years
before Jesus

SALOMÉ
Married to **Zebedee**
Mary's Sister-in-Law
born 5 years
before Jesus

Mary's Nephews and Jesus' Cousins

JUDE
THADDEUS
a Disciple
born 8 years
after Jesus

JAMES
The GREATER
a Disciple
born 13 years
after Jesus

JOHN
The EVANGELIST
a Disciple
born 15 years
after Jesus

JAMES
he LESS
Disciple
rn 8 years
ter Jesus

JOSEPH
born 10 years
after Jesus

SIMON
ZEALOT
a Disciple
born 12 years
after Jesus

JUDE
born 14 years
after Jesus

The Story of Mary

The Story of

The Mother of Jesus

by LOUIS M. SAVARY

Illustrations by RITA GOODWILL

THE REGINA PRESS
New York

Contents

To Parents and Teachers

My primary intention in writing this book is to show children that Mary was a very real and believable human person, like the rest of us, even though she was very special.

Since the New Testament writers offer no information about Mary's life before the Annunciation and very little about it afterward, I have had to rely for many elements of her story on ancient texts such as *The Protogospel of James*, *The Gospel of the Infancy*, and *The Passing of Mary*. Unfortunately, these texts are a blend of sometimes contradictory folklore and popular tradition.

Since I am writing for children and not an audience of scholars, I have chosen not to present comparative versions of Mary's story for the young reader to sift through and choose from. Instead, in the light of research currently available, I have assumed the responsibility of making choices of detail and interpretation at each step along the way, and to invent dialogue in order to present a naturally flowing and coherently believable story of Mary.

For authentic descriptions of daily life in the Palestine of Mary's day, I am grateful for research done by many scholars, especially Henri Daniel-Rops and Frances Parkinson Keyes.

For Mary's geneology I have followed the version presented by the eminent French scholar, Emile Rey, officially approved by the Vatican and accepted by the White Fathers in charge of Saint Anne's sanctuary in Jerusalem. It is interesting to note how the Ministry of Jesus was so closely connected to his family. For instance, at least five of Jesus' apostles were probably his first cousins.

From time to time in the text I insert expressions such as "it seems" or "probably" or "we are told," to remind the reader that many details of Mary's story taken from popular tradition are not unshakeable historical facts.

It is my hope that in this telling of Mary's story children will come to know and love her in a more personal way.

Louis M. Savary, PH.D., S.T.D.

Mary is Born

The Beginning

The story of Mary is the story of a person who loved God with all her heart and mind. She was a child whom God loved. And she was chosen to be the mother of God's son, Jesus.

Mary's Mother and Father

We are told that Mary's parents' names were Anne and Joachim. When they were children, both Anne and Joachim lived in Nazareth. Both their families were good neighbors, so Joachim and Anne knew and loved each other for a long time.

Happily Married

After Anne and Joachim married, they came to live in Jerusalem with Anne's family. Her father was called there to hold a position in the Temple.

In Jerusalem, Anne and Joachim continued their life together. As the years went by, their lives remained happy and abundant.

They loved books and music. We are told Anne used to sing and Joachim played the harp.

One Thing Missing

Although they were prosperous and happy, one thing was missing in their lives. They were married almost twenty years, yet they had no children. They were sad about that. Some people mistakenly thought that not having children was a sign of God's disfavor.

A Girl Is Promised

One day Joachim was alone in the fields praying that God would give him and Anne a child.

An angel of God appeared and told Joachim that God heard his prayer.

"You and Anne will have a daughter," God's messenger said. "She will be devoted to God from her childhood and be filled with the Holy Spirit

from her mother's womb. She will be called Mary and will be blessed above all women.''

That same day God's angel gave Anne the same message he gave Joachim.

When Joachim came home that evening, they told each other what they heard the angel say.

Happily and eagerly, they waited for the daughter God promised them.

A Girl Is Born

Some months later, Anne gave birth to a baby girl. They gave her the name Mary.

Mary was a very popular name in those days as it still is today. The name means royal incense, a special kind of incense used in the temple to worship God.

Presenting Mary to God

Anne and Joachim promised to dedicate their child to God. They reminded each other that God gave them Mary as a special gift.

Soon after she was born, they carried her to the great Jerusalem Temple and presented her to God.

A Birthday Party

On Mary's first birthday, Joachim and Anne held a big party for her. Though she was too young to realize it was her birthday, Joachim invited all his friends from the Temple to celebrate with him and Anne in their home. Mary received many gifts, including toys and clothes.

Mary Goes to School

Going to School

We are told that when Mary was three years old her parents took her to the Temple School for girls in Jerusalem. There, near the great Temple, she would live and work and study until she was fourteen years old.

It was a special privilege to go to this school. Only daughters of the priests and Temple officials were allowed to attend. Mary's father Joachim was a Temple official.

Mary's mother probably went to this school, too, when she was young because her father also was a Temple official.

Learning the Bible

Sitting on low stools with the other girls in her class, Mary learned about the God she loved so much. She listened to stories about God's plans for the Jewish people and God's promise to send her people a savior.

Using the Bible as a textbook, their teacher also helped them study history, geography and mathematics. Almost all of Mary's schooling was based on the Bible.

In class she and the other girls also studied music, learned to dance and recited psalms.

A Day at School

Living at Temple School she had many duties besides her school work. The women teachers showed her how to cook, sew and perform other household tasks.

During the day, there would be times set aside for prayer.

And at night, when Mary finished all her duties, prayers and studies, it was time for bed. She took her sleeping mat rolled up against the wall and spread it on the floor. Then she blew out her small oil lamp and lay down to sleep.

Weaving the Temple Veil

While Mary was attending school, the great Temple in Jerusalem was being rebuilt. The task called for thousands of workers. It was a project started by the Roman King Herod.

Each week caravans came to Jerusalem carrying rare stones, precious woods and large quantities of gold and silver into the Temple courtyard.

Working on large looms, Mary and the other young girls helped weave the colorful veil that would hang in the Temple sanctuary. She would be proud of having helped to make something for the new Temple.

The solemn dedication of the new Temple took place when Mary was about ten years old. She was probably present with her family.

Mary and Her Parents

Mary's mother and father could visit her often at Temple School. Her mother helped her with studies.

Mary also could spend time with her parents at their home in Jerusalem. They probably spent her vacation times at their other home in Nazareth.

During the months Mary was in school, her parents stayed in Jerusalem. They wanted to be close to her because they loved her and she was their only child.

Moving to Nazareth

When Mary was fourteen years old, she said goodbye to Temple School and to her friends there.

It was expected that all of the girls who finished Temple School that year would soon be getting married.

In those days a girl's parents usually selected the man she married.

We are told that Anne and Joachim decided to move back to Nazareth and make that their regular home. Perhaps there they hoped to find a husband for Mary.

Mary's House

Nazareth was a village on the slopes of a hill. Mary's house was probably one large room built into the rock of the hillside. This main room was covered with a flat roof that served as a sitting room or a porch. During hot summer nights, the roof was also used for sleeping.

To one side of the main room was the kitchen area with an oven and a grill. Nearby they kept bottles, baskets and large earthenware jars for storing grains, fruits and vegetables. Mary and her mother were in charge of the kitchen.

19

On the other side of the room were wooden chests. In them Mary and her mother kept their robes, veils, mantles, tunics and belts. Sometimes these chests were used as tables.

Mary's Clothing

Like all Jewish women of her time, Mary wore two layers of clothing. Beneath her outer robe she wore a shift, which was a loose-fitting dress. Over that she draped her robe and tied it with a belt. In summer, her robes were made of linen cloth and, in winter, of wool.

She had a veil for her head. Jewish women never went out in public unless their hair was covered.

Sometimes Mary wore sandals made of leather, but most of the time she walked barefooted.

A Day with Mary

Early every morning, carrying a large earthen-ware jar on her head, Mary walked to the well at the center of their village. While waiting her turn to draw water from the deep well, she chatted with the other women.

When she returned home, her mother had the stove warming. Together they baked their daily bread, using the water Mary brought, and corn-meal or barley meal which they kept in another jar.

During the day, they would wash, clean, card, and spin new wool, or they would do some dyeing or weaving.

In the late afternoon, they would begin the long task of preparing the evening meal.

Mary Gets Married

Mary's Decision

While Mary and her mother cooked, washed clothes, weaved, or mended things, they talked about Mary's future.

Anne was surprised when Mary told her she did not want to get married. Mary said she preferred to live alone, the way she had at Temple School.

Anne told Mary that Jewish people felt the Messiah was soon to come. "Because you are a descendant of David," Anne explained, "you are among the young women who might hope to become the mother of the Savior."

23

Mary held firmly to her decision. She wanted to remain a virgin. Yet she knew whatever happened to her was up to her mother and father.

With God's Help

Mary's mother and father discussed Mary's wish. They wanted to respect her decision, yet they still wanted her to get married.

"With God's help," said Joachim, "perhaps we shall find a way to do both."

Looking for a Way

Joachim went to see his younger brother Jacob, who was Mary's uncle. While Joachim lived in Jerusalem all these years, Uncle Jacob took care of family affairs in Nazareth. He was a carpenter.

The two men talked about Jacob's oldest son, Joseph, Mary's cousin. Though older than Mary, Joseph was a quiet and shy man, and a carpenter like his father. He was known as Joseph the Just because of his honesty and fairness.

The two men recalled how Joseph and Mary always seemed to like each other whenever Mary was on vacation from school and the two families were together.

A Good Idea

That evening Joachim said to Anne, "I have an idea. Since you and I have no son of our own, our nephew Joseph is our natural heir. He will inherit all we leave behind. He would be the perfect husband for Mary."

"Yes," said Anne, nodding in agreement. "Joseph and Mary have known and loved each other for a long time as cousins. Mary would be happy with him."

"Even if she intends to remain a virgin," Joachim added, "she will need to be committed to a man who will keep her and care for her."

To the delight of Anne and Joachim, both Mary and Joseph liked the idea and so did Joseph's parents.

Talking Together

We can imagine that Mary and Joseph fully discussed how they wanted to live.

Mary told him she wished to remain a virgin as she was at Temple School. "I want to dedicate my life to God, Joseph," she said.

Joseph agreed they could continue to love each other as they always did as cousins. "When we are married," he said, "I will also protect you and care for you."

A Betrothal Ceremony

A betrothal is like getting engaged to be married. For the Hebrews, however, it was a very serious event and almost as binding as a marriage.

Relatives from both families came to the betrothal ceremony which began at Mary's house. While the guests were eating, drinking, singing and dancing, Mary remained in her room until it was time for the ceremony.

A year later would be the formal wedding. Until that time, according to custom, Mary continued to live with her parents.

God's Angel

One day shortly after the betrothal, a special thing happened to Mary. While she was praying, God's angel came to tell her that God chose her to be mother of the Savior.

Mary told the angel she did not know how this could happen since she already had promised God she would remain a virgin and never have children.

But the messenger said she was not to be afraid. She would give birth to God's son through the power of the Holy Spirit and still remain a virgin. The baby was to be named Jesus.

Then Mary said, "Let it be done to me just as you have said." She agreed to be Jesus' mother.

Telling Her Mother

Mary ran to tell her mother about the message from God. They hugged and kissed each other. They praised and thanked God for remembering their people.

Anne looked at Mary lovingly. "How happy I am," she said, "to know that my daughter's child will be the long-awaited Messiah, the Savior of the World."

Mary was eager to tell Joseph. She hoped he would be happy to hear about the baby.

Telling Joseph

When Mary told Joseph she was going to have a baby, Joseph was confused because he knew it was not his baby.

His mind was troubled and he did not know what to do. Because he loved Mary very much, he wanted to believe what she said about the baby. But he found it hard to do so.

When he was alone, he thought about breaking their engagement. But if he accused Mary of having someone else's baby, Mary would be punished severely by the law. He did not want that to happen.

Joseph's Dream

After a long struggle in his mind, Joseph finally decided to have Mary sent away quietly to some relatives to have her baby, as the law allowed.

But the very night he made this decision, even before he had a chance to tell Mary, Joseph had a dream.

In the dream, an angel appeared and told him it was all right to marry Mary because her child was indeed God's own son, the Savior promised to their people.

The Happy Couple

Excitedly next morning Joseph hurried to tell Mary about his dream.

Anne and Joachim were very relieved when they heard the young couple talking happily and making plans.

Then Mary and Joseph went to tell Joseph's mother and father about Mary's message and Joseph's dream, so that Joseph's parents would understand about the new baby.

A Problem

Soon the other villagers in Nazareth would be able to see that Mary was expecting a baby. The problem was whether she should continue living with her parents, or should she now move in with Joseph's family as was the custom.

A Solution

Mary solved the problem by suggesting she visit her cousin Elizabeth in the village of Ain Kerem, a few miles from Jerusalem.

God's messenger had told Mary that Elizabeth was soon to have a baby, even though she was almost too old to have one.

It would give Mary and Elizabeth a chance to talk to each other about their special babies. And Mary could help Elizabeth get things ready for her child.

An Enjoyable Trip

As a fourteen-year-old girl, Mary would never have been allowed to make the journey to Elizabeth's village alone, so her mother and father agreed to go with her.

"It's been a long time since we've been back to our house in Jerusalem," Anne said to Joachim.

"I also have some business to take care of in Jerusalem," said Joachim. "Besides, it's spring

and a good time for us to do some traveling.''

Their trip took about five days and they enjoyed walking together in the lovely, warm air with new flowers blooming along the way.

Visiting Cousin Elizabeth

In the late afternoon, Mary and her parents reached Jerusalem and the house where Mary was born.

Next morning Mary walked by herself the last few miles to Elizabeth's house in Ain Kerem.

Elizabeth was happy to see Mary. "It is good to know you will stay with me until my baby comes," she said.

Mary and Elizabeth enjoyed one another's company. Like devout Jewish women, they prayed together and praised God for loving their people and caring for them.

Together they went often to the great Temple, especially during the holy days. Since Elizabeth's husband, Zachary, was a priest there, he could take them whenever they wished. Mary could even visit her former teachers at Temple School.

Mary and Elizabeth were busy and happy together preparing for Elizabeth's baby.

A Marriage Ceremony

Mary returned to Nazareth for her marriage to Joseph.

On the day of her wedding Mary, the bride, and Joseph, the groom, walked together in a procession from her family's house to his family's house. There, they and all the relatives who had come from far and near listened as a scribe read the marriage contract.

After the wedding ceremony, there was a big dinner party. Many times during the meal, relatives and friends arose to recite a blessing on the new couple.

After the meal, the party went on for many hours. As long as there was wine left to drink, people stayed to sing and dance and rejoice with the bride and groom.

Settling Down

Mary and Joseph decided to make their home in Nazareth. Joseph found plenty of work as a carpenter and they bought a small house of their own.

During the day, while Joseph worked in the carpenter shop, Mary was busy preparing what she would need for her new baby. Her mother helped her make baby clothes and blankets.

During the evenings, because it was a small village, Mary and Joseph went visiting. Sometimes they would visit Mary's parents, sometimes Joseph's parents. They were learning to be a new family and good neighbors.

Mary Becomes a Mother

An Announcement

Everyone was surprised one day when Roman soldiers on horseback rode into Nazareth. They announced that Caesar Augustus, the Roman king, had ordered a population count of the whole empire.

The king's order was that every man was to return to the hometown of his tribe and be registered without delay.

Joseph, being from the tribe of Juda, would have to go to Bethlehem to register and be taxed.

"What will we do, Joseph?" asked Mary. "It's wintertime and Bethlehem is a five-day journey from here."

"The journey must be made," he replied sadly.

Leaving Nazareth

Mary wanted to be with Joseph, so they decided to leave for Bethlehem as soon as possible.

"Let's hope we can return to Nazareth before the baby is born," said Joseph.

Mary hurriedly packed their warm, wool clothes and other things in travel bags. Joseph tied these bags and some of his carpenter tools on their donkey's back. He left room on the donkey so Mary could ride most of the way.

Mary kissed her mother and father goodbye. She told them to watch over the house while they were gone. They left their summer clothes, the rest of Joseph's tools and all their belongings in their new house.

"We'll be back in a few weeks," they told everyone.

A Crowded Town

As Mary and Joseph entered the town of Bethlehem, they realized many other travelers had arrived before them. Every room in the town was filled.

Suddenly, Mary realized she would soon be ready to give birth to her baby.

Joseph quickly went from house to house in this strange town. He wanted to be a good husband and find a quiet, clean place to welcome Mary's baby into the world.

Sadly, he came back to tell her that all he could find for shelter was a stable—a cave dug from the side of a hill and used for keeping animals.

Mary told him not to worry.

Both of them had wanted to have a special place for the birth of the Messiah. But now it was clear that a stable was all they were going to find.

Jesus' Arrival

After the baby was born, she hugged and kissed him. She put him into Joseph's arms so he could hold him, too.

Then they wrapped him in a soft blanket, Mary sang lullabies to him, and put him down to sleep in a manger filled with hay.

A Change of Plans

Because Jesus had been born in Bethlehem, Mary
and Joseph had to change their plans. They knew it
wasn't wise to return to Nazareth until both Mary
and the baby were stronger and more able to travel.
So they decided to stay in Bethlehem for a while.

Joseph was glad he had brought some of his
carpenter tools. He could find work in Bethlehem
to support his family while they were there.

The First Surprise

In those first days after Jesus was born, there were many surprises in store for Mary and Joseph.

First, shepherds came to visit them. The shepherds told Mary that a choir of angels appeared to them during the night announcing that the Messiah was born in a stable.

"We have come to see this special child," they said to her. "We brought him some gifts."

When Mary showed them the baby Jesus, the shepherds were delighted. She thanked them for their gifts.

And when they left the stable, they loudly proclaimed the glory of God to all the people they met.

More Surprises

A short time later, Mary and Joseph made the morning's journey from Bethlehem to the Temple in Jerusalem to present Jesus to God. It was the law that a first-born Jewish boy must be consecrated to God.

They were walking through the Temple courtyard to the place where they could buy two turtledoves as an offering. An old man named Simeon walked up to Mary, blessed the baby and asked to hold him.

When Simeon handed Jesus back to Mary, he told her that Jesus was destined to bring about the rise and fall of many Jewish people. "He will be rejected by numbers of his people," said Simeon sadly.

Looking directly at Mary, he said, "And a sword of sorrow will pierce your own heart."

Before Mary and Joseph took a few more steps, an aged, holy woman of the Temple walked up to them, looked at Jesus, and began praising God.

Then the woman turned to the people passing by and began to speak prophecies about Mary's child.

Although Mary wondered how this holy man and holy woman knew about Jesus, she treasured every word they said about him.

Still Another Surprise

When they returned to Bethlehem, another surprise happened. Three wise and wealthy men from Persia appeared at the doorway of the place where Mary and Joseph were living.

They had traveled hundreds of miles, riding on camels, to see "the new King," as they called Jesus.

They treated him like a king, too. From their luggage on the camels' backs they brought out gifts of gold, frankincense and myrrh. They placed them at the feet of Jesus, just as they would do for a king.

When Mary and Joseph asked the wise men how
they found their way to Bethlehem, they said they
followed a star that appeared in the sky.

Two Warning Dreams

Then, even more surprising things happened.
The night the wise men were planning to leave
Bethlehem, they were warned in a dream not to go
home by way of Jerusalem but to take another
highway. They obeyed the dream.

Soon after they left, Joseph had a warning dream, too. An angel in the dream told him to take Mary and the child and flee to Egypt. The reason was that Herod, the Roman ruler in Jerusalem, was trying to kill the child who was supposed to be the new king and savior of the Jewish people.

Mary and Joseph were now accustomed to having God's messages come to them in dreams and visions.

Saving the Baby

In the middle of the night, Mary and Joseph quickly tied on their donkey's back what belongings they could, leaving everything else behind. Their first concern was to save Jesus' life.

Long before the sun rose, they were on the road to Egypt. Mary held the baby close to her body, to keep him from getting chilled in the cold, damp air.

Sad News

News travels fast. Mary and Joseph were on their journey only a few days when word came that King Herod had ordered his soldiers to kill all male children in Bethlehem under two years old.

Mary then realized that if they had delayed in Bethlehem only a few days, Jesus would have been killed. Mary shivered as she sensed the danger to Jesus.

As she wept for all the mothers whose children had been murdered by Herod, she could feel the sword of sorrow piercing her heart. For the first of many times she would recall the words of Simeon in the Temple.

A Message to Nazareth

As the holy family began the long journey to Egypt, over three hundred miles away, Mary thought of her parents.

Mary and Joseph asked some travelers to tell their families in Nazareth that they were on their way to Egypt and did not know when they would return.

The travelers promised to deliver the message. Mary hoped they would keep their promise for she worried about her mother and father. She wanted them to know she was safe, together with Joseph and baby Jesus.

Many Questions

As they traveled farther and farther away from their country, Mary had many things to think about.

"How strange are the ways of God," she thought. Only a few weeks ago she and Joseph set out from Nazareth expecting to return there soon. Now, on the unfamiliar road to Egypt, she wondered if she would ever return to Nazareth. Would she ever talk with her mother and father again and see her friends?

And why had God let his own Son be born in a stable? Why did God first announce Jesus' birth to poor shepherds? Why did God give the sign of the star to gentiles, the Wise Men? Wasn't Jesus supposed to be a Savior for the people of Israel?

And Egypt. Why Egypt? How would she and Joseph manage to live in Egypt? Would they find people there who spoke their language? Would Joseph be able to find carpenter work? Would they find a house to live in?

Mary's mind was filled with many questions.

Called Back from Egypt

As far as we can tell, Mary and Joseph lived with Jesus in Egypt for at least a few years. Then God's messenger came to Joseph in a dream. The angel said now they could return to the land of Israel safely because the king who wanted to murder Jesus was dead.

Returning Home

As they journeyed back to the land of Israel, Joseph and Mary thought they would like to live near Jerusalem, perhaps even in Bethlehem.

But Joseph was told in another dream to settle farther north. So they decided to go back to the town of Nazareth where they had been married.

Sadness and Rejoicing

When the Holy Family walked into Nazareth and went to see their families, there was both sadness and rejoicing.

The sad news was that Mary's father Joachim died while they were in Egypt. People said he died of sadness and worry over Mary, his only daughter, who left Nazareth and never returned. The message that travelers brought him about her going to Egypt worried him all the more. "How much he loved her," is what people said.

Mary loved her father very much, too, and she cried when she heard of his death.

46

Meeting Grandmother Anne

There was much joy in Nazareth, too, for Mary's mother Anne was there to greet the weary travelers.

Mary used to tell Jesus about his Grandmother Anne. Now at last he was receiving her first hugs and kisses.

Mary used to tell Jesus stories of the Jewish people. Now Grandmother Anne would also tell him stories about his grandparents and their families.

Mary Raises Her Son

Feeding Her Family

Very soon, Mary was used to living in Nazareth again. Early each morning she would hurry to the town well with her jar and carry home the water for drinking and cooking.

Almost every day, while Joseph was at work and Jesus at school, she would bake bread or biscuits.

On market days, Mondays and Thursdays, Mary would go to buy food for her family. Although they seldom ate meat, they did have fish. At the market there were plenty of fresh fruits and vegetables.

When Jesus came home from school, he would be hungry. Mary might surprise him with a sweet treat of bread covered with honey. Then she would send him off to play or to be with his father at the carpenter shop.

Celebrating Passover in Jerusalem

Each year Mary and Joseph took Jesus to Jerusalem to celebrate Passover. This was the holy day that reminded the Jewish people that, with Moses as their leader, God brought them out of slavery in Egypt.

Mary reminded Jesus that they also spent time in Egypt. Like the people in Moses' time, they too were called back by God to live in the land of Israel.

Whenever they came to Jerusalem, they stayed at Grandmother Anne's house, the house where Mary was born.

Telling Stories

When they were together in Jerusalem, Mary and Anne probably told Jesus stories about the marvelous things that happened when he was born and the prophecies that were spoken about him.

They told him that God was his father. Jesus liked to call God his Daddy. In their language, the word for daddy was "Abba."

Mary took Jesus to the Temple and showed him around. She pointed out the Temple School where she lived and studied when she was his age.

Most of all, Jesus liked to listen to the teachers in

the Temple courtyard as they told stories and discussed the Bible and the law.

A Large Caravan

When Jesus was twelve years old, Mary and Joseph took him with them to Jerusalem for the Passover. As usual, they traveled with a large caravan of others from Nazareth. Each family found its own place to stay in the Holy City. Mary, Joseph, and Jesus would stay with Grandmother Anne, for she was now living in Jerusalem again.

At the end of the weeklong feast, all the Nazareth families assembled at a certain gate and began the journey northward toward home, over sixty miles away.

A Lost Son

Mary and Joseph presumed that Jesus was with them in the Nazareth caravan going home.

"He's probably with the other young people," they said to each other.

It was not until the caravan came to rest for the first evening that they discovered Jesus was nowhere in the Nazareth group.

They were very frightened. They decided to return to Jerusalem the next morning to look for

their lost son. It was too dangerous to travel after dark.

They spent a sleepless night in camp and early next morning hurried back to Jerusalem.

Looking for Jesus

Back in Jerusalem, they searched frantically but could not find him. They also went to Grandmother Anne's house to see if she had heard anything of Jesus.

We can imagine Anne may have assured them that the boy was all right because he came to spend the night at her house.

"He told me he was listening to the teachers in the courtyard," Anne said. "He's probably back there with the teachers now."

Mary and Joseph hurried to the Temple. There in the courtyard they saw him.

How confident and grownup he looked, sitting among the Doctors of the Law, listening to them, asking questions and answering their questions as if he was an equal.

Mary's Response

Mary cried with relief when she saw Jesus. She went up to him and said, "My son, why have you done this to us? How worried your father and I have been in our search for you."

"Why were you looking for me?" Jesus replied. "Do you not know I must follow the call of my Father?"

Mary did not fully understand what he was saying but she felt sorrow pierce her heart again. She realized one day her son would leave to do the work ordained by his Father.

Back in Nazareth

Mary, Joseph, and Jesus then went back to Nazareth where they continued to live.

When Jesus was not in school, he worked with his father and learned to be a good carpenter.

As Mary cooked their meals and mended their clothes, she prayed to God for her son. He was a good son and a hard worker. But she knew in her heart that one day his heavenly Father would call him again.

But years went quietly by and there was no call.

Mary and Jesus Alone

We are told that during those quiet years Grandmother Anne died, and so did Joseph.

When Joseph died, Jesus observed the thirty days of mourning for him required by the Law. For three days he did not work, and each day afterward he said special prayers in Joseph's honor.

Then Jesus took his place as the man of the house.

Jesus continued the family tradition of his father, working in Nazareth as a carpenter. Mary continued caring for the house.

Sometimes, when Jesus recited his daily prayers facing Jerusalem, Mary watched him and was very proud.

Jesus was constantly at the center of Mary's thoughts. Each day Mary wondered if this would be the day he would leave. But still there was no call.

Stories About Cousin John

Mary and Jesus heard stories about a certain man named John who was baptizing people in the River Jordan.

They found out it was cousin John, son of Elizabeth and Zachary. In fact, some of Jesus' cousins, Aunt Salomé's sons, James and John, became followers of John the Baptist.

The White Cloak

For some time Mary was weaving white cloth to make a cloak for Jesus. The cloak was very distinctive because it was white and because it was made in one piece, without a seam. When he wore it, it would mark him as someone special.

Saying Goodbye

One day after Mary gave Jesus the white cloak, he came to her wearing it. He said he was going to see cousin John the Baptist.

Mary knew his time had come. She was sad to see him go, but she knew God had something important for him to do if he was to be the promised Savior.

She kissed him goodbye and cried when he left. She would miss him.

Hearing About Jesus

As weeks went by, Mary heard stories from villagers and travelers that Jesus went to visit John the Baptist, that the Baptist was imprisoned by Herod the Roman ruler and that Jesus was beginning to preach and teach in the villages of Galilee.

Mary heard that Aunt Salomé's sons, James and John, were following Jesus now that the Baptist was in prison. Some fishermen from Bethsaida also became his disciples.

Mary Goes with Jesus

Going to a Wedding

After a time, Mary had occasion to see Jesus again because both of them were invited to a wedding in Cana, a village near Nazareth. Jesus brought his new disciples with him. He wanted them to meet his mother. All sat near each other at the wedding.

Right at the happiest part of the wedding feast, Mary noticed that the wine was running short. She felt badly for the new bride and groom for they would be embarrassed to tell the guests there was no more wine to drink.

Not knowing what to do, she told Jesus of the problem.

He said, "We should not interfere. Besides, my time has not yet come."

But her pleading look said to him, "We must help the embarrassed couple."

Jesus smiled back at her.

Mary signalled the waiters to come and told them, "Do whatever my son tells you."

Jesus quietly performed his first miracle just because his mother asked him. He turned water into wine. The only ones who knew about the miracle were Mary, the waiters, and Jesus' new disciples.

A Proud Mother

After the wedding, Jesus and his mother together with the new disciples, walked to Capharnaum, where one of the disciples, Simon Peter, had a home.

During the week that they stayed there Mary heard Jesus teach in the synagogue on Sabbath. The people were deeply impressed with his words.

Then she watched as he cured a man possessed by an evil spirit and, later on, at Simon's house he cured Simon's mother-in-law of a high fever.

After supper, people from Capharnaum brought other sick people to see Jesus and he cured them all.

Mary was proud of her son and she could tell that the people of Capharnaum truly loved him.

But when Jesus suggested they return to Nazareth for a few days, Mary was not sure how people there, in the village where he was brought up, would receive him.

A Worried Mother

In Nazareth, Jesus went to the synagogue on the Sabbath as usual and he stood up to read.

Mary was there and so were all their relatives, watching and listening.

From the scroll of the Prophet Isaiah, Jesus read about the coming of the Messiah. When he finished reading, he looked at the people and announced that Isaiah's prophecy was now fulfilled.

Then the people angrily arose in the synagogue and said, "You are not the Messiah! We know who you are! You are only the son of Joseph the carpenter!"

Some wanted to chase him out of town and some were so angry they wanted to flog him publicly. It was unheard of for anyone to claim to be the Messiah. Luckily, Jesus slipped away from the angry crowd.

Sitting in the synagogue after everyone stormed out, Mary felt frightened for her son. When he was a baby she remembered how the Roman king wanted to kill him. Now his own villagers—and even some of his relatives—wanted to do away with him. Again, Mary's heart was filled with sorrow.

Embarrassed and Angry Relatives

When the people of Nazareth heard that Jesus
continued to preach, some of his relatives were
even more embarrassed and upset than ever. They
made plans to stop him from preaching and acting
as if he were the Messiah. They decided to go and
talk some sense into him.

They persuaded Mary to come with them when
they confronted Jesus.

When Mary and the upset relatives reached the edge of the crowd where Jesus was teaching, they passed a message through the crowd to Jesus.

"Your mother and your relatives are standing outside the crowd and want to talk with you," was the message.

It seemed that Jesus knew what was on the minds of his relatives and he refused to see them. Instead, he continued speaking to the crowd.

Jesus said, "My real family are those who hear the word of God and put it into practice."

Then the relatives left angrily, but Mary was proud of her son and stayed on to help him.

Helping Jesus

Not all of the relatives disliked Jesus. In fact, as we know, some of them were his disciples. Some of their mothers traveled with the group, too.

For example, there was Jesus' Aunt Salomé who was married to Zebedee, the fisherman. Salomé and her two sons, James and John, walked with Jesus. Aunt Mary, who was married to Cleophas, helped out, too. She also had two sons who were Jesus' disciples. They were Simon the Zealot and James the Less. And Uncle James' son, Jude Thaddeus, was a disciple.

Mary was grateful for the relatives who helped Jesus and were as proud of him as she was.

But Mary was still anxious about Jesus' safety. Jesus was loved by all who believed in him because he healed them in body and soul. But she knew the Jewish officials were angry at his claim to be the Messiah and wanted to put him to death.

To Jerusalem

Mary overheard Jesus telling his disciples how dangerous it would be for them in Jerusalem, especially during Passover time. But still he wanted to go. So all went with him.

When they arrived in Jerusalem, Jesus knew someone who had extra rooms large enough for the whole group to use privately.

Mary worked with the other women to prepare all the necessary food for the Passover meal.

A Dangerous Night

This night would never be forgotten. Mary could feel the danger. She could not get rid of an anxious feeling all during the meal, while she and the other women sat quietly in the next room to where Jesus and the disciples were eating. At meals like this, the men and women ate in separate places.

After dinner, the men went out for a walk. Mary helped the women clear away the food and get the rooms ready for everyone to sleep that night.

Mary could not rest. All the women were worried because it was late and the men had not yet returned home.

An Arrest

Imagine their terrified shock and surprise when, in the dead of night, some disciples burst into the room announcing that Jesus had been arrested.

Mary's heart skipped a beat. She grew cold with fear.

Hidden in the Crowd

Next morning, Mary stood hidden among the crowd of angry Jews outside Pilate's palace. She saw her son paraded in front of the jeering mob. She saw his bruised and bloody body and the crown of thorns on his head. She heard her own people shouting, "Crucify him, crucify him!"

She could not stop crying.

Again a sword of sorrow pierced her heart as she heard the Roman governor give in to the crowd's verdict and issue the order: "Crucify him!"

Waiting on the Road

Mary waited along the narrow roadway where she knew her son must pass on his way to the Hill of Calvary. She had to see him, if only for a moment. Her look would reassure him she loved him with all her heart.

No words were spoken between them as Jesus, with a cross on his shoulder, slowly moved by his mother.

As he passed out of view, she remembered the words he spoke to her the day she found him in the Temple when he was twelve years old: "Did you not know I must follow the call of my Father?"

On Calvary Hill

Mary made her way through the angry crowds to the top of Calvary Hill. She watched as they nailed her son to the cross and then lifted it so he would hang and die in front of everyone. She saw her son's cross placed between two criminals.

The sword of sorrow pierced her heart again and again.

Mary saw the soldiers take all of Jesus' clothing and divide it among themselves. When they examined his white cloak and saw that it had no seam, they decided not to tear it. Instead, they threw dice to see who would win it as a prize.

Mary watched a young soldier win the white cloak she had woven for Jesus with her own hands.

Standing by the Cross

After a while, when the crowd was under control, the soldiers let a few of Jesus' friends and relatives stand near the cross.

Mary, his mother, was there with John, the disciple Jesus specially loved. Also, there were Aunt Mary, the wife of Cleophas, Aunt Salomé and other women of their group.

Listening to Jesus

Mary listened closely to each word Jesus spoke from the cross.

Seeing his mother near John, Jesus said to her, "Woman, this is your son," and to John, "This is your mother."

Jesus wanted his mother to know that she would be cared for after he died.

Holding Her Child

We are told that at the moment Jesus died an earthquake took place and darkness covered the land. In Jerusalem, because of the quake, the veil that hung in the sanctuary of the Temple was torn from top to bottom. This was the same colorful veil that Mary helped to weave when she was a child in Temple School.

After Jesus died some men took him down from the cross and gave him to his mother to hold. Mary held her child's lifeless body in her arms. Once more, the sword of sorrow pierced her heart.

By now her heart, like the sanctuary veil, felt as though it had been torn from top to bottom.

Mary Helps the Christians

Hiding in the Upper Room

After the burial, everyone gathered in the upper room to keep the Sabbath. All were sad and afraid.

The disciples were afraid that what happened to Jesus would happen to them if the Jewish officials found them.

Mary and the other women mourned and prayed. And even though Mary told everyone that Jesus would not abandon them, it was hard for them to feel hopeful.

A Special Visit

We are told by many that on Easter morning, before anyone else knew that Jesus was risen from the dead, he appeared privately to his mother Mary.

She had been faithful to him all his life. Now he graced her with the fullest realization that he was God's own son.

By Easter Sunday evening, everyone in the upper

room was rejoicing in the risen Lord. Mary, too, rejoiced with them and she praised God for glorifying his son.

At Home in the Upper Room

Mary remained in Jerusalem with most of the other women. The upper room became a sort of home for the disciples and the women who traveled in their company. It seemed they would be staying there for several weeks. Jesus frequently appeared there to teach the disciples.

One day when he had come to teach them, Jesus and the disciples walked over to Bethany, a section of town just outside Jerusalem. There, Jesus was lifted to heaven by God. It was the end of his time on earth. But he promised to send them the Holy Spirit and to be with them always.

Waiting for the Holy Spirit

The disciples returned to the upper room and began to pray for the coming of the Holy Spirit.

Mary and the other women were among them, encouraging everyone to remain fervent in prayer.

Ten days later, on Pentecost, when they were all together in the upper room praying, the Holy Spirit came down upon them like a blowing wind with tongues of fire. All were filled with the Holy Spirit.

Meeting New People

On Pentecost, Mary watched the disciples go out bravely into the streets and tell people about her son, Jesus. Many who heard began to believe in Jesus as the Messiah.

Through the next weeks and months, new converts came to meet and talk to each other. Many wanted to meet Jesus' mother, Mary.

They asked her questions about Jesus' birth and childhood, questions only she could answer. She told them of the visions, dreams and prophecies about Jesus.

Mary was very much at the center of the new Christian community and the upper room became their headquarters.

Mary was careful to watch that none of the new believers who came to the upper room went away hungry or in need. It was a rule among the early Christians that those who had things would share them with those who did not.

With John

John, the disciple, remembered Jesus' request that he take care of Mary, so she went to live in his home. When John went on missionary journeys, we are told, Mary lived with his parents Zebedee and Salomé, in their home beside Mount Olivet.

Talking About Jesus

Wherever Mary was, the new Christians came to visit her and talk with her about Jesus.

Luke, a physician who became a disciple of Jesus, often asked Mary to tell stories about how Jesus came to be born and what he was like as a child.

When Luke wrote his gospel of Jesus for the world, he included many of the stories Mary told him about Jesus' birth and childhood.

To Be with Jesus

About two years after Jesus ascended to heaven, we are told, Jesus appeared to Mary in a vision telling her she would soon die. And like him, she would be taken in her body to heaven.

Mary asked that the apostles be with her at her death. And they were all able to be present.

When Mary died, we are told, her body glowed with great brightness and the air was filled with the fragrance of lilies.

The apostles carried her to the tomb, they kissed her for the last time and departed.

After they left, Jesus appeared, called her by name from the tomb and embraced her.

Then the angels came and escorted Mary to heaven to be with Jesus and the Father forever.

Remembering Us

We are told that when Mary came into paradise, she was crowned Queen of Heaven in the presence of all the angels.

Now in heaven, she continues to take care of all her children, all on earth who ask for her help.

Till the end of time, countless blessings will come to us from Jesus because of the loving care and concern of Mary.

PRINTED IN BELGIUM BY

proost

INTERNATIONAL BOOK PRODUCTION

a chart

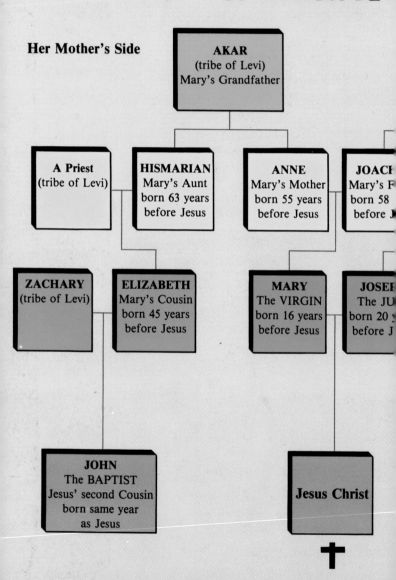

Her Mother's Side

AKAR
(tribe of Levi)
Mary's Grandfather

A Priest
(tribe of Levi)

HISMARIAN
Mary's Aunt
born 63 years
before Jesus

ANNE
Mary's Mother
born 55 years
before Jesus

JOACH
Mary's F
born 58
before J

ZACHARY
(tribe of Levi)

ELIZABETH
Mary's Cousin
born 45 years
before Jesus

MARY
The VIRGIN
born 16 years
before Jesus

JOSEF
The JU
born 20 y
before J

JOHN
The BAPTIST
Jesus' second Cousin
born same year
as Jesus

Jesus Christ

†

Adapted from the geneology by Emile Rey.